Continuing Courtship

- A Date Activity Resource for Couples -

January–December:
52 Planned Date Activities

Brandon and Danielle Porter
Marriage Built to Thrive

© 2018 Centered Simplicity, LLC
All rights reserved.
ISBN: 9781792900945
Independently published

Contents

Welcome!	i
Making the Most of Date Night	ii
Making Date Night Happen When Kids are in the Picture	iv
– JANUARY –	1
New Year's At-Home Date	2
Beat the Winter Blues	4
Monthly Game Night Date Night	6
Mediocre Poetry Night	7
– FEBRUARY –	9
Groundhog Day At-Home Date	10
Valentine's At-Home Date	13
Your Inner Artist At-Home Date	15
How Well Do You Know Your Spouse? Date Night	17
– MARCH –	19
Cookie Competition & Salsa Sampling At-Home Date	20
Something New for Dinner Date	21
Luck of the Irish At-Home Date	22
Basketball Date Night	23
– APRIL –	25
Head, Hand, and Foot Massage Night	26
Concert, Symphony, or Comedian Date	27
Childhood Date	28
TED Talks At-Home Date	29

– MAY –   30
    A Date Night in Mexico   31
    Sports Spectating Date   33
    Relive a Decade At-Home Date   34
    Picnic at the Park   36

– JUNE –   37
    Hit a Bucket of Golf Balls Date   38
    Tourists in Our Own Town Date Night   39
    The Sandlot Summertime Date   40
    The Western At-Home Date   41

– JULY –   43
    Celebrating the Nation's Birthday At-Home Date   44
    Fun in the Water   46
    Classic Board Game Tournament   47
    The Value Dollar Date   48

– AUGUST –   49
    Summertime Outdoor Amusement   50
    Something New for Movie Night   51
    Mini-Golf with Consequences   52
    Take a Walk, a Ride, or a Hike   54

– SEPTEMBER –   55
    Nostalgic After School At-Home Date   56
    Do-Good Date   57
    Child-Designed Date   59
    New Games to Play At-Home Date   60

– OCTOBER – ... 61

- Showtime Date Night ... 62
- The Mystery At-Home Date ... 63
- Indoorsy Camping ... 64
- Harry Potter Halloween At-Home Date ... 65

– NOVEMBER – ... 67

- Get to Know You More At-Home Date ... 68
- Spare Change At-Home Date ... 69
- Pie Night Group Date ... 73
- Acquire Sweet Skills At-Home Date ... 74

– DECEMBER – ... 75

- Paper and Pencil At-Home Date ... 76
- *Home Alone* & *Elf* At-Home Date ... 79
- Holiday Options Date ... 81
- Snolf or Mini-Golf at Home ... 84

– FIFTH FRIDAYS – ... 86

- A Walk Down Our Memory Lane Anniversary Date ... 87
- Card Bowling & Dessert ... 89
- Dinner Drawn Out of a Hat ... 90
- Your World of Books Date ... 91

Welcome!

Congrats on taking the initiative to continue your courtship! By using these date activities, you can nurture and fortify your marriage as you continue to make great memories together, deepen your connection, and strengthen your friendship!

These date activities are intended to be fun, budget-friendly, and practical—most can be done at home. Each date activity includes conversation starters to help you continue learning new things about each other, no matter how long you've been married (you may be surprised by what you learn)! Be sure to review the date activity details before your date night to identify and obtain any materials you may need. Be sure to make these date activities your own by adapting and customizing them based on your personalities, resources, and environment. We hope these ideas can spark your own creativity!

Who We Are
We're Brandon and Danielle Porter. We've been having a good time as husband and wife for 14 years. We have six children, so we appreciate simple and reasonably priced out-of-the-house dates and quality at-home date activities. We've also done enough schooling to appreciate what research brings to the discussion of how to build thriving marriages (we both received bachelor's degrees from Brigham Young University, and Brandon obtained a master's degree in family and human development and a PhD in education, both from Utah State University). These factors have come together in creating this dating resource—something fun, practical, and beneficial for couples!

Making the Most of Date Night

The following steps will help you succeed in using dates to continue your courtship:

Plan: Success begins by putting the date night on the calendar. This increases the likelihood that the date will happen and sets the time apart from other time you spend together throughout the week. Calendaring the date gives you an event to look forward to, which can be especially helpful during some challenging weeks. It can also help both of you feel that you and your relationship are being invested in and valued. Strive for consistency—a weekly date is recommended, though near-weekly dates will benefit your marriage, too.

Once the time is set, decide who will take the lead for planning the date activity. Take advantage of your creative energy while you have it by planning the date activity earlier in the week. The planning process can be made easier by having a list of date ideas to choose from. That's where this resource comes in! As you will see from these ideas, the planned activities don't have to be over-the-top or expensive to be high quality and enjoyable.

For bonus points, occasionally ask or text the question, "Will you go on a date with me this weekend?" Doing so can rekindle good feelings and bring sweet validation to your spouse.

Add a Little Novelty and Variety: Dinner and a movie can make for a nice date night. If you've been consistent with this approach and it's something you both enjoy and that helps you connect, well done. If there are other date activities that you like repeating together, keep them going!

Your continued courting can bring even more rewards to your marriage by adding a little novelty and variety to your date activities. Research shows that sharing new experiences can result in added excitement, connection, and positivity in your relationship. Novelty and variety can come by making simple variations to date activities you've already done or by trying new activities together (and "new" doesn't have to mean extreme or far outside of your comfort zones). This date activity resource is designed to help you make this happen!

Date Well: With an enjoyable activity planned, be intentional about being a good date. Choose to be fully attentive—mentally and emotionally present. Talk together and help your spouse have a good time as you do the same!

Date Night Game Changers
1. Put the date on the calendar and plan the activity.
2. Try something a little different or new.
3. Be engaged on the date and have a good time!

Making Date Night Happen When Kids are in the Picture

As our family has grown, we've dealt with the challenge of wanting to make consistent dates happen but not knowing how to do it without breaking the bank on babysitters. Setting aside money for babysitters and date activities has been helpful, as have the following budget-friendly approaches:

At-Home Dates
Use fun date activities that can be done at home after your kids have been put to bed. For the at-home dates in this resource, you can avoid staying up too late by including your kids in the dinner portion of the date.

If your kids generally stay up late, you can put on a movie for them in one room and enjoy your date in a different part of your apartment or house.

Near-to-Home Dates
As your oldest child is getting to the point of being able to watch his or her younger siblings, near-to-home date activities can get you out of the house for a short time and allow for a speedy return if needed.

Over time, you may be able to rely more on one of your children to be the full-fledged babysitter. As payment, consider giving the child "credits" toward an event that he or she is interested in, such as a summer camp or a sport.

Babysitting Swaps
Approach #1: Get together with several families who have children that are similar in age to your own. Rotate babysitting each week, with all of the children going to one couple's house for the night. With four families involved, you get three free date nights each month!

Approach #2: Similar to Approach #1, but arrange a swap with only one family once per month.

Approach #3: Parent-as-babysitter swap. In this approach, the date begins later in the evening after you have put your children to bed. An adult friend (who has children) comes over to sit with your sleeping children—a low-demand babysitting situation—while you and your spouse go out. You then swap with the couple on another night.

Family Members
Some couples live close enough to trusted family members to tap into their babysitting services. Just be considerate and thoughtful in asking!

– JANUARY –

New Year's At-Home Date

(Start the year off right with this great at-home date!)

Boost Your Endorphins Spend at least 10–15 minutes working out together. Consider a few rounds of jumping jacks, pushups, crunches, and stretches. Or, search online for a simple cardio or weightlifting workout. Some great workouts are available for free at FitnessBlender.com.

"Dear Us" Write a simple letter to yourselves to open on January 1 of the following year (a little humor is encouraged in writing this ☺). Include the following:
- A funny or memorable memory worth preserving and recalling from the previous year.
- A list of fun activities you plan to engage in this year as a couple and/or family.
- Your forecast for how your marriage will grow throughout this year.
- A few lines about how you each feel about the other.
- Anything else you feel inclined to write.

Put the letter in an envelope and seal it. Or, save the letter on a computer and place a reminder on your digital calendar on January 1 of the following year to check the letter.

Couple's Bucket List Create, or review and update, a marriage bucket list (things you want to accomplish as individuals and as a couple in your lifetime).

New Year's At-Home Date (continued)

Resolutions Share your individual resolutions for the new year and discuss how you can support each other in accomplishing them.

Inspire Greatness If you're in the mood for a movie, tap into the "inspirational" genre. We recommend the Oscar winning *Rocky*!

Treats To promote New Year's wellness, eat nuts and try a new recipe for fruit smoothies. Or, search online for other tasty "healthier than normal" treat options and try something you find.

Start the Conversation

What is one New Year's resolution you have accomplished in your life?

At what times in your life have you been grateful for a new start?

Beat the Winter Blues

(Obliterate any blues brought on by the middle of the winter season with this fun at-home date! We've had a great time doing this as a group date.)

Prepare to Laugh Prior to the date, both of you find 7–10 hilarious YouTube clips. Think of commercials, stand-up comedy bits, comedy skits, movie scenes, 80s music videos, human errors, funny things kids do or say, sports bloopers, or pranks. (If you need help getting started, email us and we will send you a list of five winning clips from times when we've done this as a group date night.)

Watch and Laugh Have a good time watching the clips together. If you want to watch your clips without ads or items in the sidebar, search online for "watch YouTube videos without ads." Select one of the websites that provides this service and enjoy!

Treats Treat yourselves with ice cream with your own mix-ins, such as crushed up candy bars, fruit, nuts, syrups, or whip cream!

Start the Conversation
When have you laughed hardest in the past three months?
What is the funniest movie you've ever seen?
If a video clip were to be made of one of the funniest moments in your life, what moment would it be?

Beat the Winter Blues (continued)

Group Date Variation
If done as a group date, be sure you have a large viewing area and a large screen (we've used a projector to project onto a wall).

Submissions Prior to the event, each couple needs to submit 3–5 of their funniest (and group-appropriate ☺) YouTube clips to you as the hosts. View the clips and create categories (e.g., Stand-up & Comedy Sketches, Commercials, etc.) and a voting card with each clip listed by category.

Watch, Laugh, and Vote Give everyone a voting card and something to write with. Watch one category of clips, then instruct everyone to vote on their favorite from the category. Repeat for each of the categories.

And the Beat the Winter Blues Emmy Goes to… Gather the voting cards, tally the votes, and give awards to the winners!

Treats Ask each couple to bring a treat to share.

Monthly Game Night Date Night

(Fun, easy to plan at-home date!)

Select the Game Select one game that you both would enjoy playing once each month for at least six months (we've chosen games like Six Card Golf, Nerts, and Catan).

Play the Game Enjoy playing the game together (play several rounds of it if it's a shorter game). Keep an ongoing tally of your scores or a record of who wins each time you play.

Repeat Next Month and the Next and the Next... Play this same game once each month for a date night, building on the previous months' win totals or scores. It's fun to see how you can lose and regain ground over the course of months! To add some variety in subsequent months, consider playing fewer rounds of your monthly game and add in different card or board games. Keep track of the outcome of these games as well.

Determine the Winner At the end of six months, post the Game-Night-Date-Night overall winner in your home or on social media!

Treats Popcorn or chips and soda are great game-night treats!

Start the Conversation
What is a personal accomplishment that you're secretly quite proud of?
If you had more spare time, what is something you would choose to do?

Mediocre Poetry Night

(How long has it been since you wrote your last poem? In this at-home date, aim to craft the most mediocre and humorous poetry possible. Drop a line, attempt to rhyme, all while not taking yourself too seriously ☺.)

Poetic Primer To prime your poetic skills, both of you look up or recite from memory two of your favorite poems (think Shel Silverstein, Edgar Allen Poe, Robert Frost's "The Road Not Taken"). Discuss what you remember about learning or hearing the poems and anything you like about them.

Rhyme Time Select a random topic for you both to attempt to write a rhyming poem about, such as "drivers who don't use their blinkers" or "80s music." Read for each other what you create. Repeat this process for another random topic, such as "junior high school" or "my favorite pair of pants."

Poetic Variety Select a random topic, such as "our neighbor's pet" or "selfies." For this topic, both of you write a different type of poem, such as haiku, limerick, or free verse (search online, if needed, for instructions on these different forms of poetry).

Grand Finale Write one final poem, in whatever form you choose, about your spouse. (You could consider doing acrostic poems for this one.)

Public Vote If you're feeling brave, post one poem from each of you on social media and ask your friends to vote on their favorite for "most mediocre poem"!

Mediocre Poetry Night
(continued)

Treats Something refined is most fitting for this poetic occasion. Slice up a baguette and place salami and cheese on top. Add some sparkling juice in fancy glasses.

Start the Conversation
What was the first poem you memorized?

If you could become gifted in one form of art, such as poetry, painting, or sculpting, which would you choose and why?

– FEBRUARY –

Groundhog Day At-Home Date

(Groundhog Day isn't the most nostalgic of holidays, but the movie provides great inspiration for a fun date night!)

Breakfast for Dinner As inspired by the diner breakfast scenes in *Groundhog Day*, make breakfast for dinner!

Something Worth Repeating Imagine waking up to the same song every day! Each of you search online for an oldie song that you wouldn't mind waking up to every day for a week. Share what you find. Do this same thing with a modern song and with a song from a movie soundtrack that you could wake up to.

Have fun with at least two of the following activities:

> **Mastering a Skill** In *Groundhog Day,* Phil uses his time loops to learn different skills—piano, ice sculpting, and French poetry—to impress Rita. Split up and take a few minutes to learn a simple skill to impress your spouse with help from an online tutorial. Some skills to consider: hand lettering, moonwalking, KonMari clothes-folding method, making a bed properly, or making a napkin rose.

> **Improved Efficiency** By repeating the same day over and over again, Phil eventually increases his "living efficiency." Do the same with a level or activity on a video game (something like Mario Kart or Just Dance). If you don't have a video game system, pull up a Just Dance video on YouTube. Do the level, activity, or dance 2–3 times and see whose efficiency improves the most with repetition!

Groundhog Day At-Home Date (continued)

Jeopardy Master One of the best scenes in *Groundhog Day* is when Phil watches Jeopardy and wows the others in the room with his knowledge. Create your own similar Jeopardy experience by doing the following:

- Each of you list 4 topics you feel you could ace trivia about with Phil-like confidence, such as a favorite sports team, fast food burgers, an actor or actress's career, a holiday, a book series, a musician, musicals, or a hobby.
- For each topic selected by your spouse, search online to come up with 4 clues in the form of answers, Jeopardy-style. Assign each clue for each topic a money value, such as $100, $200, and so forth, based on the difficulty of the clue. (Note: This is a smaller game board than is traditionally used in Jeopardy. It took us about 25 minutes to come up with the clues for each other in this simplified form, but the end result was worth it!)
- Draw a Jeopardy board for your spouse, using the topics as the categories. Designate one spot as a Daily Double. (Prior to responding to this clue, whoever is answering will need to place a wager up to the maximum of his or her present score.)
- Take turns selecting a clue and answering (switch roles when an incorrect answer is given), tracking the points for correct responses given in the form of a question.

Groundhog Day At-Home Date (continued)

Cards in the Hat To have fun while passing time one night, Phil and Rita flick playing cards into a hat. Do the same by setting a hat on the floor and mark the spot you'll throw from. Use two decks of cards with different markings (one for each of you), or split one deck of cards by suit color. Give yourselves one warm-up round and then compete to see who can toss the most cards, one card at a time, in the hat!

Watch the Flick Sit back and enjoy watching *Groundhog Day*! If you don't feel like watching the entire movie, search online for your favorite scenes and watch those.

Treat Inspired by one of Phil's meals at the diner, enjoy either donuts or cake for your movie treat!

Start the Conversation
What is one part of today that you wish you could have done over?
What is one day of your life that you would want to relive?

Valentine's At-Home Date

(Nothing like a little friendly competition to sweeten up your Valentine's season!)

DIY Conversation Hearts Create two original, home-made conversation hearts for each other. To make them, cut four large hearts out of paper (two for each of you). Come up with your own conversation-heart sayings, and put them on display!

Compete against each other in several of the following events:

> **Hugs & Kisses Unwrapping** While wearing oven mitts, take turns trying to remove the wrappers on as many Hershey Hugs or Kisses as possible in one minute. Do a few rounds.
>
> **Heart Stacking** Competing at the same time, both of you stack as many candy conversation hearts as possible using only one hand. Whoever has the highest standing tower at the end of one minute wins! Make this a best-of-three competition.
>
> **Q-Tip's Arrows** Place a bowl or container in the middle of the table or floor and mark a shooting line. Take a straw and a pile of Q-tips. Competing at the same time, try to shoot your "arrows" (Q-tips) into the bowl by placing a Q-tip in the straw and blowing it out.

Valentine's At-Home Date (continued)

Name That Couple Working individually, select five movie couples. Come up with three clues hinting at the identity of the couple, such as where the couple lives, events in the couple's story, something one of the characters said, and so forth. The third clue should provide a strong probability of guessing the couple correctly ☺.

To play, one of you begins by giving the first clue for the selected couple. If whoever is guessing identifies the couple after the first clue, he or she receives 3 points (if after the second clue = 2 points; after the third clue = 1 point). Alternate back and forth repeating this process until each couple has been guessed. Highest score wins!

Dance Floor All to Yourselves Dance to 3 or 4 slow songs in your kitchen or living room.

Romantic Snippets If you're in the mood to watch something, search online for movie trailers or clips of favorite scenes from some of your favorite romantic movies. Enjoy what you find!

Treats Snack on some of the items used during this date, or make your own chocolate-dipped strawberries.

Start the Conversation
What are some of your positive memories of past Valentine's Days?

Your Inner Artist At-Home Date

(No matter which side of your brain dominates, you'll find the ability to have a good time with this date!)

Portraits On individual slips of paper, write different mediums, such as crayons, colored pencils, and markers (or whatever supplies you have on hand). Each of you select a paper without looking. Using your selected medium, sketch a portrait of your spouse's face.

Scenes from Our Story Pull out some playdough (store-bought or homemade—it's pretty easy to make). Each of you recreate some location that has significance to your relationship and see if the other can guess what it is. (If you don't have any playdough, each of you draw the location you thought of using a different medium from what you used on the portraits. Set a time limit of 3 minutes for an added degree of difficulty.)

Art Critics Search online for famous works of art (see some suggested works below). Each of you share your thoughts regarding why you think that piece of art became famous. Or, look up the art of Norman Rockwell and discuss what you enjoy about his works.

> Suggested works: *The Starry Night* (van Gogh); *Paris Street; Rainy Day* (Caillebotte); *Whistler's Mother* (Whistler); *A Sunday Afternoon on the Island of La Grande Jatte* (Seurat); *The Night Watch* (Rembrandt)

Your Inner Artist At-Home Date (continued)

The Joy of Painting **with Bob Ross** Search online for an episode of "The Joy of Painting" with Bob Ross. (Don't brush this off—you might be surprised at how enjoyable this is!) Using water colors, try to paint along for a while with Bob. Or, go outside and paint a landscape of your choosing.

Treats Enjoy some cheese, crackers, and grapes.

 Start the Conversation
What childhood experiences with drawing, painting, or playdough do you remember?
If you could have one scene from your life depicted in art, which would it be and why? How would it look?
Is it best for an artist to provide the interpretation of his or her creation, or to allow viewers to interpret it themselves?

How Well Do You Know Your Spouse? Date Night

(Over time, you've had the opportunity to learn a lot about each other. Now is the chance to put your knowledge to the test!)

My Spouse Would Like… For dinner, go out to eat and order for each other. (If you can tell your spouse is way off from what you would want, helpful hints are allowed ☺.)

I Knew Just What You'd Want… Go to a superstore—one that includes grocery and retail items (or adapt this for a store that is conveniently located near you). Each of you take a shopping cart. Separate and select the item from the following list that you think your spouse would choose for himself or herself:

- Sugar Cereal
- A decoration for your home
- Potato or tortilla chips
- Toy figurine
- Salad dressing
- T-shirt
- Spread for bread
- Scented candle
- Book or magazine
- Frozen dinner

Meet back together and explain your selections. Have fun discussing what you got right and where you were way off as you return the items to their shelves. Consider purchasing one of the items as a souvenir from your date!

How Well Do You Know Your Spouse? Date Night (continued)

A Treat We Can Agree On Pick out a treat that you both would like for dessert. Take it home and enjoy!

 Start the Conversation

What is something fun that you have learned about me that you didn't know when we got married?

How have some of your interests changed throughout our marriage?

– MARCH –

Cookie Competition & Salsa Sampling At-Home Date

(Tastiness abounds in this date!)

Cookie Baking Contest Prior to the date, both of you select a new cookie recipe and get the necessary ingredients. Start off your date by making the cookies together. While the cookies are baking, snack on the salsa (see below).

To avoid personal bias in judging whose cookie is the tastiest, take a few of each type of cookie to a neighbor for a taste test. They should be happy to help! (If you choose to decorate your cookies, have your neighbor select the "best decorated" as well.)

Salsa Sampling Prior to the date, purchase 3–4 different types of salsa. Enjoy taste testing the different salsas. Determine which is "most unique," which is "most likely to be forgotten," and which is "most likely to be purchased again."

Cookie Drop Put several cookies on a plate. Leave them anonymously with a nice note on the doorstep of a neighbor who would appreciate a little love.

Start the Conversation
What foods did you not like as a child but you now enjoy eating?
What is the best meal you have ever had?
What meal would you be okay with having once a week for the rest of your life?

Something New for Dinner Date

(Add some novelty to going out to eat by trying one of these simple ideas.)

Friendly Recommendations Text or talk to some neighbors or friends and ask them for restaurant recommendations. Or, search online for the top restaurants in your area. Try something new!

New Cuisine Do you usually go to out for Chinese, Mexican, or Italian food? Try a Japanese, Thai, or Greek restaurant.

Food Truck Fun Search online for "food trucks near me." See what, if any, food trucks are close to you. Select one and enjoy!

New from the Same Go to a favorite restaurant, but order something new. You could try a new entrée, get appetizers for your main course, or get a dessert you've always wanted to try.

Roof-top Takeout Picnic Get takeout and eat it picnic-style on your roof. If you live in an apartment, eat on the balcony or on the living room floor, or ask some friends if you can borrow their roof!

Start the Conversation
What were your family's eating-out habits growing up (e.g., how often, favorite restaurants, etc.)?
If you could host any three people who have ever lived, or who are presently living, for dinner, whom would you invite?
If you opened your own restaurant, what type of food would you serve? What would your restaurant be named?

Luck of the Irish At-Home Date

(Bring out your green and your luck for this fun at-home date!)

Irish Carving Each of you get a bar of Irish Spring soap and a butter knife or short paring knife. See what you can carve up!

Lucky Charms Eat a bowl of magically delicious Lucky Charms!

Lucky 21 Play the card game 21 (search online for instructions, if needed) and see who has the best luck. Play the best-of-seven.

Taste the Rainbow Place a bowl of Skittles in the middle of the table. Place a cup on each side of the bowl. Each of you select a color of Skittles and place a straw in your mouth. Going at the same time, race to see who can remove more of their Skittles from the bowl into their assigned cup in one minute by sucking up one Skittle at a time. Try a second round using different colors!

An Irish-ish Flick Watch a movie connected in some way to Ireland, such as *The Quiet Man* with John Wayne. Or, watch clips from Riverdance's Official YouTube Channel. For a fun Riverdance spoof, search online for the first performance of Stavros Flatley on Britain's Got Talent and enjoy!

Treats for the Show Enjoy green ice cream (mint or lime)!

Start the Conversation
What's a time when you were lucky as a child? As a teenager? What are some ways that you consider yourself lucky now?

Basketball Date Night

(Minimal basketball skills are required for this fun at-home or near-to-home date!)

Find the Court Locate a basketball hoop close to your home, such as at a nearby park or playground, a neighbor's driveway, or your own (if you have one ☺).

Play the following games, and any other games you would both enjoy. If one of you has a significant advantage, consider shooting with your non-dominant hand.

> **H-O-R-S-E** Search for instructions online, if needed.
>
> **Around the World** Use sidewalk chalk to draw on the ground the markings found around a basketball key. After each made basket at a designated spot, advance to the next spot. When the spouse who shoots first misses, the other spouse begins his or her turn until he or she misses. The first spouse then resumes from the last spot he or she missed from. The first to make it "around the world" wins!
>
> **7 on the Line** You each begin with seven points. If whoever shoots first makes it, there is 1 point "on the line." If the second shooter also makes the shot, there are 2 points on the line. If the first shooter then misses, he or she loses 2 points (because there were 2 points on the line). The line is then "cleared." If the shooter misses after the line is cleared, no points are lost because there were no points on the line. Continue until one of you loses all of your points.

Basketball Date Night (continued)

Spectators of the Game Return home and enjoy watching a college or professional basketball game. Or, watch a basketball movie like *Glory Road, Hoosiers,* or *Space Jam.*

If you time this date with the beginning of the NCAA men's college basketball tournament, complete tournament brackets and enjoy the added fun of watching to see if your teams win!

In-Game Snacks Dunk cookies in milk and make homemade nachos or popcorn.

Start the Conversation
What are some of your basketball-related memories?
What, if anything, have you learned about life from sports?
Describe a funny, awkward, or embarrassing sports-related memory from your past.

– APRIL –

Head, Hand, and Foot Massage Night

(Time to relax and acquire some gifts that keep on giving. Note to husbands: Foot massages are an especially good gift for pregnant wives...and non-pregnant wives.)

Set the Mood Put on some relaxing "spa" music to set the mood for the date, or put on any music that you both enjoy.

Head Massage Search online for "how to give a head massage." Find a helpful video to watch, or select a website that has instructions and practice on each other. For added relaxation, place your feet in a tub or in buckets of warm water (use Epson salt or bubble bath for extra luxury).

Hand Massage To refresh your hands after their hard work on the head massages, search online for "how to give a hand massage." Learn and practice on each other.

Foot Massage Remove your feet from the water and dry them. Search online for "how to give a foot massage." Review the instructions and practice on each other's nicely relaxed feet.

Treats A massage night calls for chocolates and berries.

Start the Conversation
What is your favorite way to relax at the end of a long day?
What are 3 of your favorite smells?
What are 3 of your favorite sounds?

Concert, Symphony, or Comedian Date

(Good music and laughter can create great memories!)

Identify Your Options Prior to the date night, identify venues in your area where concerts, symphonies, or comedian performances are held. Look online to see who is performing and when. If you live near a college or university, you could look into a concert put on by a campus-based performance group. You could also look ahead to summertime to identify local outdoor concerts.

Or, think about some of the musicians, bands, or comedians that you both enjoy. Check their tour schedules to see if they have anything planned near to you during the year. (Put performances that interest you on the calendar for future date nights!)

Enjoy the Show Enjoy being entertained by gifted performers!

Bring the Comedian Home If there aren't any concerts, symphonies, or comedian performances that interest you this month, find a comedian's routine on DVD from your local library or on an online streaming service and watch it at home.

Treats Get some ice cream bars you've never tried–the fancier the better!

Start the Conversation
How have your music tastes changed during your life? What's your go-to song for putting you in a good mood? What's one of your favorite all-time jokes (or at least one that you can remember)?

Childhood Date

(These childhood activities were fun then and make for a great date night now!)

Childhood Fine Dining Go out for grown-up versions of some of your favorite meals as children, or make the meals at home. For example, gourmet mac and cheese in place of boxed mac and cheese, or chicken tenders or wings in place of frozen chicken nuggets. Or, go to a fast food restaurant and get kids' meals, as well as another regular item or two off the menu (just to be sure you get enough to eat ☺).

Arcade Battle Go to an arcade that has ticket-winning games. Have a competition to see who can earn the most tickets! Consider setting a rule that each game can only be played up to four times. Compete for the highest score in other games as well.

Brain Freeze Buy slushee drinks on your way to the park or your home. Or, stop by a gas station or convenience store and purchase the treat that you would have picked out as a child.

Kites or Sidewalk Chalk At a park or in an area near your home, try to fly a kite (if you've got some wind). Or, create a mural on the sidewalk with sidewalk chalk. (You could even look up some simple pointers on sidewalk chalk art—it's a real thing!)

Start the Conversation
What hobbies did you have as a child?
What sayings did your parents use with you while you were growing up?

TED Talks At-Home Date

(The internet provides access to incredible amounts of information and entertainment. Combine the two in this date by taking advantage of TED talks!)

TED Talks TED talks are short talks that pack powerful and insightful messages. Either prior to your date or at the beginning of it, each of you search TED.com for one or two talks that interest you. Watch or listen to them together and discuss your thoughts about what's presented.

(Note: One alternative is to do something similar with podcasts that you are interested in. You can find great podcasts on a variety of topics, such as marriage, parenting, finances, organization skills, and more.)

Puzzling While listening to your TED talks, do a puzzle together. If you feel like investing a little and plan ahead, you can use an online service to make a puzzle with family photos.

Treats Munch on some of your favorite nuts!

Start the Conversation

If you were to ever give a TED talk, what would your topic be?

What are two or three personal, family, or work challenges that you need to solve?

– MAY –

A Date Night in Mexico

(Take a trip to Mexico with this great at-home date!)

Set the Mood Search online or on a music playlist app for mariachi music. Put it on in the background.

Mexican Cuisine Make a new Mexican dish together, such as Mexican flatbread pizzas (search online for a recipe). Or, try a new meat recipe for tacos, like chili verde. Not in the mood for cooking? One of you run out and bring home your favorite Mexican food! For a beverage, make Horchata.

Habla Espanol Using Google Translate, each of you type a love note to the other person in English and read it in Spanish (bonus points for using lots of adjectives). Enjoy trying to speak this beautiful language!

Have some fun with one or two of the following activities:

>**Fun and Games** Prior to the date night, purchase a pirinola online to play Toma todo (it's like a dreidel). Review instructions online. Consider using your favorite M&Ms or Skittles for your game "tokens." Or, purchase loteria boards and cards online and play (it's like Bingo).

>**Feeling Crafty?** Try using aluminum foil and permanent markers to create your own Mexican tin art (search online for further instructions, if needed). Or, get a basic molding clay you can bake and acrylic paints to create your own colorful Mexican pottery.

A Date Night in Mexico (continued)

Dancing If you're the dancing type, search online for a tutorial on a traditional Mexican folk dance. Have a good time learning together!

Los Film Watch a movie based in Mexico, such as *Coco*, *Three Amigos*, or *Nacho Libre*.

Treats For your movie treats, go green, white, and red with some guacamole, tortilla chips, and salsa!

Start the Conversation
What is your dream vacation?

If you could have been born at this same time but in a different place, where would it be? Why?

Sports Spectating Date

(Watching sporting events in person can be a blast! Baseball, the "American Pastime," is used as an example for this date activity. You can follow this pattern for attending another sporting event that you enjoy or that you've never watched in person, like hockey or soccer.)

Find the Game Determine what options exist for attending a baseball game close to you. Look into professional league, minor league (triple A, double A, class A), college, or even high school.

Take Me Out to the Ballgame Go enjoy the game together!

Ballpark Treats If allowed, bring your own sunflower seeds, sports drink, and bubble gum to enjoy during the game.

Start the Conversation
What experiences have you had with playing baseball or softball?
What sport would be challenging for you to enjoy watching?
Have you ever won a trophy or medal? If yes, what for?

Relive a Decade At-Home Date

(Step into a prior decade of your choosing—we recommend the decade of your childhood or teenage years. Have fun rekindling memories by doing some of the following activities!)

Seconds to Name that Song Working individually, take a few minutes to select 10 popular songs from the decade you selected. One of you lead out by playing the first song on your list (use an online digital music player or online store that provides previews of songs). The other spouse tries to name the song as quickly as possible. Once the song is successfully named, write down the number of seconds it took. After going through the 10 songs, tally the total number of seconds. Repeat this process for the other spouse. Whoever has the lowest total of seconds is the winner!

The Decade's Best Dance Moves Search online together for "popular dance moves in the (decade you chose)." Go through an article and images that come up or select a video to watch and enjoy the memories that come back! (You could even attempt to (re)learn some of the dance moves ☺.)

Toys, Treats, and Trends Search online together for "popular toys in the (decade you chose)." Review the lists or images that come up. Share memories you have about some of the toys. Repeat this process for *treats* of the decade and then for *trends*.

In the News Trivia Working individually, take five minutes to search for major events in national, world, or sporting news from the decade. Create 10 trivia questions (consider making them true-or-false or multiple choice). Take turns quizzing each other.

Relive a Decade At-Home Date (continued)

On the Screen Brainstorm together some of the shows you watched during this decade, or search online for some of the most popular shows of the decade. If the shows had introduction clips, find some of them online and watch them. Discuss any memories you have involving these shows. Share what your TV watching habits were while growing up.

Next, search online together for "top grossing movies of the (decade you chose)." Watch the trailers for 2-3 of these movies online, as well as for any other movies you can remember watching and enjoying from this decade. Share memories you have related to some of these movies.

Game If you still own a game from your decade of choice, pull that out and play it. Some popular retro games are still sold, so you might be able to find one online and order it prior to your date.

Movie If you're in the mood for a movie to end the date, select a goody from the decade you've revisited.

A Taste of the Decade See if any treats from the decade you selected are still being sold in grocery stores and enjoy some of them during the date.

Start the Conversation
Conversation starters are spread throughout the activities above.

Picnic at the Park

(Fresh air adds a sweet spice to a date. Take advantage of the spring weather by picnicking and playing outdoors!)

Picnic Dinner Pack a picnic or get takeout and eat it picnic-style at a park.

Cloud Watch Lay back for a few minutes and watch the clouds. Brush off your shape-identifying abilities and point out to each other what you see.

Play Have fun playing one or more of the following while at the park (consider borrowing one of these games from a friend or purchasing your own—they can be good investments!):

Croquet	Ladder Golf
Bocce Ball	Three-Hole Washer Toss
Kubb	Catch with a football or Frisbee

Monkey Bars and Swings If the park has monkey bars, have a timed race on them. If there are swings, enjoy those as well!

Treats Eat some tasty seasonal fruit.

Start the Conversation
How did growing up where you did influence who you are?
What is the worst or most random advice you've ever received? What is some of the best advice you've received?

– JUNE –

Hit a Bucket of Golf Balls Date

(Even if you and your spouse aren't golfers, you can have a great time with this date activity!)

FORE! Find a nearby golf course that has a driving range. Go hit a bucket or two of golf balls. If you don't have golf clubs, borrow from a friend or purchase a few secondhand (or some locations may have rental clubs). If needed, watch an online tutorial together on how to hit a golf ball.

For added variety, select a target and see who can hit it. Or, track your best hits in your first three attempts. Then track your best hits in your last three attempts. Whoever has the most improvement gets to pick the place for shakes!

Putting Around If the golf course you picked has a practice putting green, have some fun putting around. See who can sink the longest put!

Treats Get fries and shakes for dessert.

Start the Conversation
What is something new you have wanted to try? Why haven't you tried it yet?
What is a skill you have that, from the outset, you were unsure whether you could develop?

Tourists in Our Own Town Date Night

(Sometimes we pay good money to see other people's towns, yet we never take the chance to explore our own! These ideas can be easily adapted in touring a nearby town.)

Local Cuisine Go to a restaurant in your city that you've yet to try.

A Little History Visit your town hall and look for a display on your city's history (or you might find some history at your city library).

Stroll Down Main Street Hold hands and stroll down your city's main street. Visit some shops or stores that you've yet to go in.

Landmarks and Statues Visit landmarks or statues around the city. See what you can learn about them (you might find some insights online).

Love Where You Live Throughout the date, be sure to take pictures of the two of you at the sites you visit. Get pictures of other places or unique characteristics of your city that you would want to remember should you ever move.

Treat Stop by a candy shop, bakery, or ice cream store that you've yet to visit and get something good!

Start the Conversation
What do you love about where we live? If you could change one thing about our city, what would it be? Would you prefer living in a small town or big city and why?

The Sandlot Summertime Date

(Set the mood for summer with this fun movie-themed date! Put on your baseball shirts and PF Flyers for added effect.)

Pre-game Meal Go out for hot dogs, or grill some of your own.

"Who's Got the Big Bat Now?" Get two rounds of batting practice in at local batting cages. In the first round, try your best to distract your spouse as he or she tries to hit. In the second round, see who can place a called shot and who can get the furthest hit. (At-or-near-to-home alternative: Take turns doing the same things using a wiffle ball and bat.)

"Just Stand There and Stick Your Glove Out in the Air" Find a large enough area to play catch with a baseball. To appreciate a beginner's experience (and for a good laugh), throw with your non-dominant arm for a bit.

"S'more What?" For dessert, make s'mores in your kitchen. Toast the marshmallows on a candle, or bake the s'mores in the oven (find a recipe online, if needed).

"Sandlot, Sandlot, Sandlot!" Watch *The Sandlot*!

Start the Conversation
What are some of your memories of summers as a child?
What, if any, neighborhood rivals when you were young? What confrontations did you have?
What's something you did as a child that got you into trouble?

The Western At-Home Date

(Cowboy hats are optional ☺.)

Cowboy Grub Make steaks, baked beans, and biscuits or cornbread for dinner.

Cowboy Wisdom While dinner is cooking, search online for cowboy wisdom or John Wayne sayings. Select your top three and share them with each other. (If you're feeling creative, prior to the date, download an old or rustic looking paper image and print a few copies. Write on the papers some of the favorite sayings you find and put the papers up around your house.)

Deadeye Set up ten candles (five for each of you) spaced a few inches apart from each other. Mark a shooting line a few feet away. Light the candles and use water pistols to put them out. Play multiple rounds from different distances. (If you're looking for some real shooting action, get some guns and go to a shooting range.)

Quick Draw Using your water pistols, face each other, count down from 3, and shoot (all in good fun ☺). Play multiple rounds.

Country Dancing Search online for a tutorial on country line dancing or country swing dancing. Have fun learning together.

A Western If you're in the mood for a movie, watch a western like *True Grit* (1969), *The Man Who Shot Liberty Valance* (1962), *McLintock*, or *High Noon*.

The Western At-Home Date (continued)

Treats Enjoy bottled root beer and your favorite jerky.

Start the Conversation
What in your personality would make you a good, or not so good, fit to be a cowboy or cowgirl?

– JULY –

Celebrating the Nation's Birthday At-Home Date

(Adapt this date using activities related to your nation's birthday. July 4, America's Independence Day, can be a busy day filled with parades, BBQs, and other activities. If you have children, after you've put them to bed, enjoy a date on July 4 by watching fireworks from your rooftop together. The following date activities are meant to be done on a different day.)

BBQ Dinner Grill some BBQ for the two of you.

Did-You-Know Toppers Each of you choose an American artifact, such as the American flag and the one-dollar bill. Search online for interesting or random facts about the artifact. Go back and forth sharing your top 3–5 "did-you-know" facts, trying for the conversation "topper" with the most insightful or random fact. Repeat the same process for the following topics: U.S. Constitution, U.S. Presidents, and American monuments.

Watermelon Stick-It Cut a watermelon in fourths and prop one piece up. Get a deck of cards for each of you, or split one in half. Take turns flicking the cards one at a time in an attempt to get them to stick into the pink of the watermelon. See who can get the most cards to stick.

Seed Spitting Cut pieces of another fourth of the watermelon and have a seed spitting contest. Compete for accuracy and distance.

Celebrating the Nation's Birthday At-Home Date (continued)

Water Balloon Target Toss Draw a large target using sidewalk chalk on the road or in your driveway. Mark the inner circle with a 50, the next circle with a 30, and the outer circle with a 10. Stand 15–20 yards away and toss water balloons at the target. Points are earned based on where the water balloons hit the target.

Water Balloon Batting Practice For added fun with water balloons, take turns pitching and trying to hit water balloons. (The spray from the exploding balloons will feel nice in the heat!)

Sparklers If allowed in your area, prior to going in for the night, have some fun with sparklers. Snap photos of attempts to make symbols or letters. (You may need to take a few practice photos to find the best setting for your camera.)

Patriotic Movie If you're in the mood for a movie, consider watching one related to America, such as *Mr. Smith Goes to Washington*, *Lincoln*, or *National Treasure*.

Red-White-and-Blue Dessert Enjoy vanilla ice cream topped with strawberries and blueberries.

Start the Conversation
How did you celebrate Independence Day while you were growing up?
What are you most grateful for about living in the United States? What do you love most about being an American?

Fun in the Water

(What's summer without some fun in the water? Choose one of the following activities that fits best with what's accessible to you.)

Swim at a Pool Dive, chat, race using different strokes, swim laps…just enjoy yourselves!

Waterpark Go ride the slides! (Both of us were surprised at how fun it was going to a waterpark with just us!) Some places offer discount prices a few hours before closing.

Go Out on the Water Rent paddleboards, kayaks, a canoe, or a rowboat and go out for a good time on a lake or reservoir.

Tube a River Floating down a river can be a relaxing and fun way to spend time together. It will take some coordinating with cars so that you're not stranded when you end your tube run ☺.

Bodyboarding If you're fortunate enough to live near the ocean, go have some fun riding waves and relaxing on the beach together.

Treats Swing by the grocery store and get popsicles, or get snow cones from a stand.

Start the Conversation
How did you learn to swim?
What childhood memories do you have of swimming pools, waterparks, or playing in lakes, rivers, or the ocean?

Classic Board Game Tournament

(Some board games never go out of style—we just forget to play them. Bring back some of your favorites with this fun at-home date!)

The Events Get a variety of classic board games that don't take too much time to play, such as Battleship, Chutes and Ladders, Checkers, Connect 4, Guess Who, HiHo! Cherry-O, Qwirkle, Scrabble, Sequence, Sorry!, Trouble, or Yahtzee.

Set the Timer Decide how long the tournament will go (we recommend 1.5–2 hours).

Compete! Play as many games as you can in the allotted time. Track the outcome of each game to determine the overall winner of your classic board game tournament!

Victory Treats The spouse who won gets to pick a treat for the other spouse to go purchase and bring back!

Start the Conversation
What cheers you up best when you're feeling down?
Name two of your pet peeves.
What predictable things about me do you appreciate?

The Value Dollar Date

(Get the most bang for your buck in this date!)

Value Menu Dinner The rule for dinner is that you can only order items off of a value menu at a favorite fast food restaurant.

Dollar Store Shopping Ask your spouse to name three numbers between 3 and 10. These numbers are the amount you have as a couple to spend. For example, by choosing the numbers 4, 3, and 9, your amount would be $4.39. Use this money to purchase something you can do together, such as a card game or outdoor toys, and a snack you can share. Get creative with your frugality!

Play Find a spot to have a good time with what you purchased!

Other Activities to Consider:
Make Your Own Mugs Purchase white mugs at the dollar store. When you get home, use permanent markers to create your own designs on the mugs. Search online for instructions on how long to let the mugs dry and bake.

Puzzle Races Each of you select a puzzle from the dollar store (be sure the puzzles have the same number of pieces). When you return home, race each other to see who can complete their puzzle first. Then switch puzzles and race again.

Discount Movie Go to a movie at a discount theater.

Start the Conversation
What is the best deal you've ever gotten on a purchase?

– AUGUST –

Summertime Outdoor Amusement

(You probably won't have to travel far to find one of the following activities that interests you both.)

Street, County, or State Fair Explore the creations, displays, and talents of your community and sample tasty treats!

Festivals or "Days" These events come in a variety of forms: community, cultural, art, theatre, hot air balloons, music, and so forth. Keep your eyes open to advertisements or search online to see what's going on nearby.

Farmers Market Shop around to see the locally produced foods and enjoy any samples that are offered. You could even purchase ingredients and make dinner together when you get home.

Rodeo Admire the awesomeness of the animals and the skill of the athletes—especially the Mutton Busting kids!

Car Show Find an outdoor car show and go admire the collection.

Carnival Head out for some rides and games!

Amusement Park Search for deals and go enjoy the thrills of the roller coasters and other rides!

Start the Conversation
Rank the top 2 and bottom 2 jobs you've had. Explain why.

Something New for Movie Night

(By the end of some weeks, a movie date night is all you need to hit the spot—and all you have energy for! Enjoy a slight twist and some practicality on movie night with this approach.)

Find the Flick Select or create a movie genre that has several movies (6–12 months' worth) within it that you both have interest in. For example:

- In the Stars (Star Wars & Star Trek)
- The Nicholas Cage Collection
- Classic Disney (e.g., *The Computer Wore Tennis Shoes, The Misadventures of Merlin Jones, The Absent-Minded Professor*, and so forth)
- AFI's 100 Years…100 Movies
- 1930s–1960s Films
- Sports Flicks
- Westerns
- Musicals
- Friends' Referrals (ask your friends about the best random movies they've seen—we'll get you started with *Lagaan*!)

Enjoy the Show Enjoy a monthly date night in which you watch one movie from your selected genre!

Treats Try a new type of popcorn or a new flavor of ice cream each month!

Start the Conversation
What is an odd or unique talent that you have?

Mini-Golf with Consequences

(An entertaining, simple variation on a traditional date-night activity!)

Get the Gum Purchase two or three packs of gum (you may want to get multiple packs of the same flavor).

Mini-Golf with Consequences Go mini-golfing, with the following variations:

>If you shoot *under* par, *your spouse* has to chew a piece of gum.
>
>If you shoot *over* par, *you* have to chew a piece of gum.
>
>For each hole, keep adding pieces of gum to your mouth based on the outcome. For example, if on Hole #1 you shoot over par and your spouse shoots under par, you must start chewing 2 pieces of gum. If on Hole #2 you shoot par but your spouse shoots under par again, you must add 1 piece of gum to what you're already chewing. (We ended up going through 21 pieces of gum between the two of us!)
>
>If one spouse has a significant advantage, he or she could golf some holes with his or her non-dominant hand.

(Note: For added variety, search online to see if there's a glow-in-the-dark indoor mini-golf course near to you. If there is, give it a try!)

Mini-Golf with Consequences (continued)

Treats Your jaws might be a little tired. Try smoothies for dessert.

Start the Conversation

When have you said something that you wished you hadn't? How did you recover?

What is one of your more (or most) embarrassing moments?

Take a Walk, a Ride, or a Hike

(Get outside and enjoy some fresh air with whichever option works best for you.)

Dinner Make homemade pizza together (consider cooking it on the grill!) and lemonade.

Take a Walk Yep, a walk around the block counts as a date. Hold hands and stroll around the neighborhood. Bring ice cream cones from home to eat as you walk (you could even make homemade ice cream if you're feeling up for it). Or, walk to a restaurant that sells ice cream and enjoy it on your stroll back home.

Take a Ride Hop on your bikes, or, if needed, borrow bikes from friends or rent bikes for an hour. Enjoy a leisurely ride together around the neighborhood or city or along a public trail.

Take a Hike If you have hiking trails nearby, take advantage of them and go on a hike (don't feel that you need to go all the way to the end of the trail for it to count ☺). If you time it right, you can enjoy the sunset.

Morning Options Dates in the morning count, too! Take a morning walk, ride your bikes to a restaurant that sells breakfast, or go for a sunrise hike.

Start the Conversation
Which three fictional characters from movies or books do you think most closely reflect parts of my personality? Describe one of the happiest days of your life.

– SEPTEMBER –

Nostalgic After School At-Home Date

(School's in! Enjoy reminiscing on what your after-school experiences were like with this great at-home date!)

Practice Many hours are spent after school in practices. Have some fun with one of the following "drills": volleyball pepper, soccer juggling, tennis volleying, or chess!

Homework Who knew homework could be enjoyable, especially when you get to pick it! Listen together to a chapter of an audio book and discuss it. Seeing that it wasn't uncommon for coloring to show up as a part of homework (even in high school), print out some coloring pages for adults, break out the colored pencils, and color while you listen.

After-School Show A little vegging could do a lot of good after a long day at school. So, find a classic after-school show (think *Saved by the Bell* or *Boy Meets World*), and watch an episode or two! Or, watch a few episodes from another show you're both interested in.

The After-School Snack There was nothing quite like coming home from school to a bowl of Fruity Pebbles! Enjoy a bowl of your favorite sugar cereals, or go with the traditional milk-and-cookies after-school treat!

Start the Conversation
What was your after-school routine like in elementary, junior high, and high school?

Do-Good Date

(Get ready for a good time doing some good together!)

Preparation Prior to the date, get $5 in quarters and $10 in one-dollar bills.

Vending and Vacuum Machines Setups Find some vending machines and leave quarters on or in them. Then drive to a car wash and place several quarters in vacuum machines so the next user will be pleasantly surprised when he or she only has to put in one quarter before the vacuum comes to life!

Grocery Store Targets Go to a grocery store and do the following:
> Gather a few stray shopping carts around the parking lot as you make your way into the store.
>
> Put-pocketing: Place $1 bills in people's shopping carts or on top of their purses as you pass by without them seeing (like when they're reaching for something on a shelf). Consider leaving the money with a post-it note that says, "You've been put-pocketed!"
>
> Buy 2 or 3 packs of gum and a sealed-package treat item, like cookies. (You'll use these later.)
>
> Before leaving the parking lot, wash the car windows of another car. Consider leaving a note behind that says, "We washed your windows. Have a great day!" Careful not to get caught ☺.

Do-Good Date (continued)

Reverse Drive-Thru Go through the drive-thru of a restaurant and order a treat for yourselves. After receiving your order, perform a reverse drive-thru by giving the worker the sealed-package treat you purchased at the grocery store as a "thank you" for what they do.

Gum Drops Select a few targets for a do-good doorbell ditch. Write, "We chews you to have a good night!" on post-it notes (cheesy, but they'll appreciate it ☺) and place them on the packs of gum you purchased. Drop the gum on the selected porches, knock, and run!

Movie If you're in the mood for a movie, consider watching a do-good movie like *The Ultimate Gift*, *Pay It Forward*, or *The Blind Side*.

Start the Conversation

What's a memorable service project that you've participated in?

What's a memorable instance when have you been the recipient of an act of service?

What other fun and simple acts of service could we do for others in the future?

Child-Designed Date

(Turn the date planning over to the kids!)

Select the Planners If you have children, turn to them to make the plan (see below). Otherwise, select young nieces or nephews, cousins, or children of a friend.

Designing the Date Tell the kids that you need their help planning a date. Ask them to give you two or three options for each of the following (be prepared to record their answers):
- ☐ What should we wear on our date?
- ☐ Where should we go for dinner?
- ☐ What should we do for an activity after we eat dinner?
- ☐ What should we have for dessert?

(Note: To make this into an at-home date, adjust some of the previous questions by asking the children to give you options for what you should make for dinner and what you should do for activities at home.)

Execute the Plan Select together from the options the children provided and have a good time!

Start the Conversation
When you were a child, what do you remember imagining being a grownup would be like?
What did you want to be when you grew up?
What do you miss about being a child?

New Games to Play At-Home Date

(We've all got games we like to play, but branch out a little for this date. For added fun, consider inviting another couple or two over to make it a group date!)

Something New with Traditional Playing Cards Message some of your family members or friends and ask them what their favorite game using traditional playing cards is. Or, search online together for a new card game and play it. Consider giving Rummy, Nerts, Golf, Crazy Eights, War, Speed, or Egyptian Rat Screw a try.

More Gaming Newness Prior to the date, purchase or borrow a new board game, dice game, or card game and play it. You might enjoy Ticket to Ride, Stratego, Farkle, Bohnanza, or Five Crowns.

Mixed-Up Chess If you need one more game to establish an overall champion for the night, try this variation of chess: rearrange the back rows of chess pieces in any order you choose and go at it!

Treats Branch out with some hummus and veggies or pita chips to munch on while you play. Or, try dipping pretzels in peanut butter or Nutella.

Start the Conversation

What was your favorite chore while growing up? What was your least favorite chore? How, if at all, have these changed over time?

What is one of the bravest or scariest things you have done?

– OCTOBER –

Showtime Date Night

(Musicals or plays may not be up everyone's alley, but you might find something you enjoy in the talent on display!)

Find the Show Search online for professional or community theatres near you and look through the musicals or plays they have scheduled (you could even look into productions put on by local high schools). Find something that matches your mutual interests and calendar. If you see any future shows that look enjoyable, put them on your calendar now.

Enjoy the Show Enjoy the talent showcased in the production! If the venue lends itself to it, dress up for the show.

Musical at Home If there aren't any productions that interest you during this month, check out a musical on DVD from your local library or rent one from an online streaming service. We recommend *Singin' in the Rain*, *Seven Brides for Seven Brothers*, *Fiddler on the Roof*, or *Newsies*.

Treats If you end up at home for the date, enjoy sliced apples and caramel dip. For added flavor, put out small bowls of toffee bits, peanuts, chocolate chips, or crushed-up Oreos to sprinkle on top.

Start the Conversation
When have you performed something on a stage?
If you could have a professional singing voice or professional dancing skills, which would you choose and why?

The Mystery At-Home Date

(Get your sleuth skills ready!)

Riddle Me This Each of you search for 3 riddles online. At different points during the date, test each other's riddle-solving skills.

Hidden Pictures Prior to the date, print off a few free hidden picture pages online (seriously, these aren't just for kids). Race to see who can find all of the items or to see who can find the most in a set amount of time. If hidden pictures don't suit your fancy, race with a few word searches.

Blindfold Taste Test There are so many options here. Prior to the date, purchase different candies (e.g., Skittles, Sour Patch Kids, Starburst, or Mambas), chocolates (e.g., Lindt Lindor Truffles or chocolates with added flavors like salted caramel or strawberry), yogurt cups, and/or mint gum (guess while kissing!). Take turns being blindfolded and sampling the different items. Compete to see who can get the most right! You could also try variations of this activity with smells (e.g., lotions, scented candles) or sounds (search online for "guess the sound").

Clue In the mood for game? Play a round of Clue!

Mystery Movie In the mood for a movie? Try watching a classic mystery like *Charade* or *Rear Window*.

Start the Conversation
What is one thing that has always been a mystery to you?

Indoorsy Camping

(Who says you have to be outside for camping to count? Transform your living room into a campsite and enjoy some of the activities you'd do while camping outdoors. Happy camping!)

Setup Set out sleeping bags (actual or make-shift), an air mattress, or even your regular mattress in your living room. For extra ambiance, set out battery-powered candles.

Tin Foil Dinners What's camping without some sort of campfire meal? Make your own tin foil dinners and cook them in the oven.

Banana Boats Slice through the top peel and banana lengthwise, but not deep enough to cut through the bottom peel. Stuff chocolate chips and marshmallows in between the two halves of the banana. Wrap the banana in foil and cook it in the oven for about 5–10 minutes at 300 degrees (until the chocolate chips are softened and the marshmallow is gooey). Enjoy!

Card Games Play a few rounds of one of your favorite card games.

Campfire Stories Tell each other your best scary campfire stories, or search online for some good ones.

Start the Conversation
What memories do you have of camping while growing up?
What's your favorite part of camping?

Harry Potter Halloween At-Home Date

(We've always associated Harry Potter with Halloween. Any muggle can enjoy this seasonal date in the world of the boy who lived!)

A Taste of Hogwarts For dinner, search online for recipes for Harry Potter foods, such as Cauldron Cakes and Treacle Tart. Make what you find, or make your own dishes and give them Harry Potter names. For example, pumpkin chocolate-chip muffins can be your version of Pumpkin Pasties.

Pumpkin Carving Test your skills by carving something Harry Potter-themed. Or, stick with a basic jack-o-lantern design if this more advanced form of carving isn't up your (Diagon) alley.

Harry Potter Trivia Come up with your own Harry Potter trivia, or purchase a trivia game online prior to the date. Or, search online for Harry Potter trivia and complete it together or test each other. While you're online, search for an "online sorting hat" quiz and see which house at Hogwarts you would each get placed in!

DIY Ollivander's Wands Prior to the date, search for small fallen tree branches that are about 10–16 inches long. Each of you pick a branch to work with and carve it into a wand that Ollivander would be proud to sell. If you're feeling especially invested, use sandpaper to smooth the wood, use a stain to color it, and spray it with a gloss sealant.

Harry Potter Halloween At-Home Date (continued)

Or, search online for DIY Harry Potter Wands to find other wand-creation options that would work for you (just be sure to get the materials before the date). For example, you can make some pretty slick wands using wood dowels, dowel caps, a hot glue gun, acrylic paints, and bronze Rub 'n Buff. (It may seem like a bit of work, but trust us, it turned out to be really fun and worth it!)

Take a Trip to Hogwarts Select your favorite Harry Potter movie and enjoy the show!

Treats Pop popcorn and make your own Butter Beer! If you're feeling brave, get a box of Bertie Botts Every Flavor Beans and try to name the flavors you eat.

Start the Conversation
What were some of your Halloween costumes growing up?

What is one of your favorite memories associated with Halloween?

If you could make one of the fantasy parts of the Harry Potter world into a reality, which would it be? Why?

– NOVEMBER –

Get to Know You More At-Home Date

(No matter how you've been married, there's still more you can learn about each other. What you learn in this date activity might surprise you!)

Personality Test Search online for a free personality test. Each of you complete the test on your own. Review and discuss your results together. Consider how understanding particular elements of each other's personalities can enhance your interactions.

Love Languages Both of you complete your love language profile at 5lovelanguages.com. Review and discuss your results together. Think about ways you can use what you learn to enhance the way you show your love to each other.

Treats Both of you list two of your favorite treats. Purchase one treat from each list and enjoy them together!

Start the Conversation

If you could change anything about your character, what would it be?

When do you need assurance of my love the most and how can I best show it?

If I could meet only one of your needs, which need would you want it to be?

Spare Change At-Home Date

(You never knew you could have this much fun with spare change!)

Gather the Coins Gather as much spare change as you can find in your home, or bring a little extra home from a trip to the grocery store. Then compete against each other in some or all of the events that follow.

Heads-or-Tails To warm up your coin-flipping skills, do 10 rounds of heads-or-tails with a quarter (each of you flips 5 times while the other spouse calls heads or tails). Make a scorecard, and give a point to the winner!

Coin Flip Set a bowl or cup in the middle of the table. Each of you take a pile of coins. Race to see who can flip three coins into the target. The first to win two rounds gets a point!

Coin Drop
Round 1: Set a breakfast cereal bowl on the floor. Place a chair backwards next to the bowl. Whoever goes first is to stand straight (no bending at the hips or knees!) on the chair with 10 coins in his or her hand. Drop one coin at a time into the bowl. After the first spouse's turn, be sure to leave any coins that stay—some may get bounced out in the next spouse's turn! After the second spouse's turn, determine who has the most coins in the bowl. Winner gets a point!

Round 2: Do the same as in Round 1, only use a cup instead of a bowl.

Spare Change At-Home Date (continued)

Coins Guessing Each of you take a pile of coins. Place either 0, 1, 2, or 3 coins in your hand without letting each other see. Each of you put your closed hand forward and call out your guess of how many coins are in the two closed hands combined (it can be 0–6). Whoever guesses second can't repeat the first guess. Then open your hands, and if one of you guessed correctly, you take all of the coins and set them to the side. Whoever wins the round gets to guess first in the next round. Play at least 10 rounds and tally the total number of coins each spouse has. Whoever has the most coins gets a point!

Coin Spinning Each of you take one of the same coin (quarters work best). Spin your coins at the same time and see whose spins the longest. Play 5 rounds. A point goes to the winner!

Penny Stacking Each of you take a pile of 20 pennies. Race to see who can stack their pennies the fastest using one hand, stacking one coin on the tower at a time. (Another option is to take turns timing each other to see who is fastest.) Give the winner another point!

Guess the Year Each of you select 10 coins. Decide who will guess first. The coin holder gives the first three numbers of the date on the first coin, such as "Nineteen Ninety…." The guesser picks a number between 0–9. If guessed correctly, the guesser gets a point. Do this for all 10 coins, and then switch roles.

Spare Change At-Home Date (continued)

Living on the Edge

Event 1: Each of you select 10 coins. Take turns attempting to slide a coin to the edge of the table without it falling off. The winner is the spouse whose coin is closest to the edge. The first to win two rounds is the overall winner and gets a point!

Event 2: Select a starting line near to the side of the table you are sitting on. Each of you place a quarter at the starting line. Race by sliding dimes, nickels, or pennies at your quarter to bump it forward and off the other edge of the table. The winner gets another point! (Another variation is to sit on opposite sides of the table. Place a quarter in the middle of the table and compete to knock the coin off the opposite end of the table.)

Event 3: Each of you select 10 coins. Stand at least five feet away from the wall. Take turns tossing a coin, trying to get it as close to the wall as possible. The first to win two rounds is the overall winner and gets a point!

Getting to a Point Get 4 index cards, and write "5 Points" on one, "10 Points" on another, "15 points" on the third, and "20 Points" on the last. Tape the cards at different spots on the table. Stand at one end of the table and take turns sliding coins to get them to land on the cards to get points (for example, if you get a coin to stop on the 10-point card, you receive 10 points). The first person to tally 100 points gets a point on the scorecard!

Spare Change At-Home Date (continued)

And the Winner Is... Add up the points. The winner gets to select the treat and the other spouse gets to go purchase it! (Or the winner can select the treat on the next date.)

Small Change If you're in the mood to discuss a book, consider the short, yet surprisingly enjoyable (even for husbands), *Small Change: The Secret Life of Penny Buford* by J. Belinda Yandell. (Read the book prior to the date.)

Start the Conversation

What are some ways that you earned money while you were growing up?

Have you ever tossed a coin in a fountain and made a wish? What do you remember wishing for? If you could toss a coin in a fountain now and wish for something, what would it be?

Pie Night Group Date

(Extend your pie eating during the Thanksgiving season!)

Pick the Partiers Prior to the date night, select 2–4 couples you would like to get together with. Invite them to come to a pie night and to each bring their favorite pie.

Get the Party Started Enjoy visiting together and consuming pie!

If it's just the two of you, do the following activities while enjoying your pie:

Candy Corn Contest For added fun during the pie night, have a contest to see which couple can place the most candy corns upright in one minute. Play a few rounds.

Expressing Thanks Write simple notes to individuals you are thankful for, such as family members, servicemen and servicewomen (current or former), teachers, or neighbors. Make these handwritten notes or send them by email, text, or through social media.

On a More Personal Note Prior to the date night, each of you write a list of 20 things you are thankful for about your spouse. Go through your lists together.

Start the Conversation
If you could eat one item from the Thanksgiving table once each week for an entire year, which would it be? What event from this year are you most thankful for?

Acquire Sweet Skills At-Home Date

(The Internet has expanded our opportunities for learning. Have a good time using it to learn some new skills together!)

Select Your Subject Think up some skills you both have interest in learning or skills that you've never really considered before but sound fun. Consider things like juggling, pen twirling, card tricks, waltzing, relaxation techniques, self-defense moves, speed reading, sketching a cartoon character, basic sign language, eating with chopsticks, chopping vegetables as seen on cooking shows, or basic car repairs.

Learn Together Search online for tutorials on 1–2 skills that you came up with. Watch, practice, and enjoy learning together!

Treats Promote your learning with tasty brain food, like Greek yogurt with berries or almonds and dark chocolate.

Start the Conversation
What makes you feel most fulfilled?
What is something interesting that you've come across in the past two weeks?

– DECEMBER –

Paper and Pencil At-Home Date

(This entire at-home date can be done with two pencils, some paper, and some dice!)

Paper Airplanes Make your best paper airplanes (consider trying some designs you can find online). Select certain targets around the room and try to hit or fly your planes through them (like a hangar hung from a light).

Hangman Take advantage of the increased vocabulary you've acquired since your earlier hangman days to make this classic game more challenging! Define upfront what parts the hangman will have, and have fun!

Paper Battleship Each of you draw two 10X10 grids on a piece of paper. Number 1–10 across the top columns, and A–J along the side columns. On one grid, lightly shade rectangles representing your fleet of ships: one 5-square aircraft carrier, one 4-square battleship, two 3-square cruisers, and one 2-square destroyer (no ships can share the same squares.) Take turns shooting at each other's battleships. Track your spouse's shots on the grid with your shaded ships, and track your shots on the other grid on your paper. The first spouse to sink all of the other's ships wins!

Letters Game Take turns naming a letter until 9 different letters are written on your paper (the same 9 letters for both of you). Work on your own to create a word using only those nine letters. (Decide together whether each letter can be used more than once.) Whoever comes up with the longest word wins the round and receives one point for each letter. Play 3–5 rounds.

Paper and Pencil At-Home Date (continued)

Guided Pictionary This is the game of Pictionary, but with a twist in coming up with the words. Both of you need to select a book. To identify your words, your spouse selects a random page number within the page range of your book. Turn to that page and count the number of paragraphs. Your spouse then selects a number corresponding with paragraph on that page. Estimate for your spouse how many words are in the paragraph. Your spouse then selects a random number in that range. That is your word to draw for your spouse to guess. Repeat this process to identify your spouse's word. (If you get the word "the," "and," or "a," select a word nearby in the sentence to draw.) Take turns drawing a picture to get the other spouse to guess the word. Play 3–5 rounds.

100-Number Dash The objective of this game is to write numbers 1–100 on your paper as quickly as possible. Play begins by taking turns rolling dice. If one of you rolls doubles, that person gets to start writing *1, 2, 3, 4, etc.* up to 100. However, that spouse only has until the other spouse rolls doubles, at which point he or she gets to take the pen and start writing his or her own list of numbers. When the other spouse rolls doubles, he or she takes the pen back and resumes numbering from where he or she left off. Continue this process until one of you has written all of the numbers from 1–100!

Paper and Pencil At-Home Date (continued)

Gomoku Draw one 19X19 grid on a paper (you will both play from this grid). Determine who is X's and who is O's. Take turns writing X's or O's on the intersections of the lines (not in the squares). The goal is to get an unbroken row of five X's or O's horizontally, vertically, or diagonally while attempting to block your spouse's efforts to do the same.

Treats Enjoy something salty, such as pretzels or cashews, and something sweet, such as candy or a quality juice.

Start the Conversation
What is your favorite way to waste time?
What is your most prized possession?

Home Alone & *Elf* At-Home Date

(Two Christmas favorites combine to inspire a great date night!)

Dinner Order a lovely cheese pizza just for the two of you, or eat spaghetti. Try a bite of noodles covered with maple syrup!

Target Practice Follow Kevin's lead and set up toy figurines on a shelf. March a few paces back and compete in target practice using a BB gun, airsoft gun, or toy dart gun. If you have snow, step outside for a few minutes, pick some targets, and see how your snowball-throwing accuracy compares with Buddy's.

Get Decorative Go to town, Buddy-style, in decorating a room in your house with homemade snowflakes and paper chains. (If you have children, they'll be impressed by the room and by the proof that mom and dad have fun dating each other!)

Indoor Sledding If you're feeling adventurous and you have enough stairs, try sliding down them on a sled or in a sleeping bag. Be sure to be careful (we assume no liability for any damages or injuries ☺) and to snap a picture!

Beverage Sampling Buddy takes Jovie to taste the world's best cup of coffee for their date, so follow suit and do some beverage sampling of your own. If coffee isn't your thing, sample different flavors of hot chocolate to determine the "world's best."

Home Alone & *Elf* At-Home Date (continued)

(Out-of-the-house option) **Ice Skating** Head to a skating rink and hold each other up as you work your way around the rink. If you feel up for it, try Kevin's technique and see how far you can slide across the ice on your knees.

Movie Treats Make a large bowl of ice cream as similar as possible to the one Kevin eats while watching his movie. Pop a bag of microwave popcorn as well.

Enjoy the Show(s) Watch some of your favorite scenes from the two movies, or select one of the movies and enjoy the entire show!

Start the Conversation

Is there a time you can remember being left behind by your parents? What happened?

If you had been in Kevin's situation as a child, what would you have done differently? What would you have done the same?

What is the best prank or trap you have heard of, done, or had done to you?

What was your best mischief moment as a child?

What brings you Christmas cheer most readily?

Holiday Options Date

(Make some fun holiday memories with the following at-home or out-of-the-house date activities that work best for the two of you.)

At-Home Options

Graham Cracker Houses Use graham crackers, candies, and white royal frosting to create and decorate graham cracker houses or villages. For the ultimate adhesive, search online for a recipe for melted sugar glue.

DIY Christmas Board Game Create your own board game by doing the following:

> Draw a path on paper with at least 30 squares from the beginning to the end (you may need to tape two pieces of paper together). Every two or three squares, write an instruction, such as "Your white elephant gift is a hit. Go ahead 1 space." Or, "You forget to buy a gift for your mother-in-law. Go back 2 spaces." Or, "You peek at your presents early. Lose a turn."

> Working individually, each of you come up with 5 Christmas-related questions in each of the following categories (20 questions total): Christmas Movies, Christmas Music, Christmas in Our Family, Christmas Other (religious elements, cultural traditions, and so forth). (Note: *If you don't celebrate Christmas, adapt some of these ideas based on the holiday you do celebrate.*)

Holiday Options Date (continued)

Select two game pieces, such as a piece of candy or a spare Christmas light, and get a die. Each turn begins by rolling the die. The spouse who rolled takes a trivia question written by the other spouse. If answered correctly, he or she moves his or her game piece forward the number of spaces shown on the die. Play until someone crosses the finish line or until you're out of questions.

Video Entertainment Pull out some old family videos from Christmases past, either from when you were children or since you've been married. Or, search online for clips from your favorite Christmas movies and watch a few.

Out-of-the-House Options
Christmas Lights Purchase hot chocolate and drive around neighborhoods looking at Christmas lights. Select your own "Best of Season" winner (you could even drop off a note or prize on their doorstep to let them know!). Or, if your city provides a light display at a central location, wander through it.

Christmas Concert or Play Many well-known and local musicians put on Christmas shows, as do symphonies, orchestras, and choirs. Some local theatres also put on Christmas-themed productions, such as *A Christmas Carol*. See what's available in your area and go enjoy the show!

Holiday Options Date (continued)

Treats 'Tis the season for peppermint or eggnog shakes!

Start the Conversation
What Christmas albums do you remember listening to as a child?
What Christmas movies do you remember watching as a child?
What sights, smells, and feelings do you remember about Christmas when you were younger?
What do you remember thinking and feeling on Christmas Eve as a child? On Christmas Day?

Snolf or Mini-Golf at Home

(Who says you need warm weather to golf?)

If you have snow where you live:
Go Snolfing! Snolf is golfing in the snow using racquet balls in place of golf balls. Select an open field area near to you, such as a public park. Dress warm and go have fun snolfing!

Design your course as you go. For example, you might tee off for the first hole at a park pavilion, hitting toward the slide, which is the "cup" (hitting the slide counts as getting the ball in the cup). The ground near the slide then becomes the spot to tee off from for the next hole, which may be a baseball backstop. Play 5–7 holes.

If you don't have snow:
Homemade Mini-Golf Set up a mini-golf course in your home! For the "cup," tape a paper or plastic cup to the floor. Work together to create 9 holes, or come up with some separately. Consider things like specific walls that the ball must bounce off of as part of the hole, placing obstructions (like stuffed animals, kids' toys, or pillows) on the floor, using toy car tracks, or starting the hole in a separate room from where the cup is placed.

You can even go for a glow-in-the-dark option. Purchase long glow stick necklaces and some bracelets. Use the glow sticks to outline the hole and the "cup." You could also use flashlights to illuminate some areas of the course.

Break out the putters and golf balls, and have fun mini-golfing!

Snolf or Mini-Golf at Home (continued)

Treats Whether you snolf or mini-golf, enjoy hot chocolate with extra toppings like whip cream, toffee bits, and caramel sauce. For added flavor, stir your hot chocolate using a peppermint candy cane! (If you go snolfing, you may want to bring the hot chocolate with you.)

Start the Conversation

If you could design the weather for 12 months, what would you choose it to be?

What do you like most about being outdoors? What do you like most about being indoors?

– FIFTH FRIDAYS –

A Walk Down Our Memory Lane Anniversary Date

(Celebrate your anniversary with this fun and meaningful at-home date! If you still live close to where your relationship began, consider taking some of these ideas out of the house.)

A Taste of Our Past For dinner, make the meal that you had on your first date or a meal that you had on one of your early dates.

Retelling Our Story Prior to the date, write each of the following phrases on individual pieces of paper:
- Retell your version of our first date.
- Retell your version of the first time we held hands.
- Retell your version of our first kiss.
- Retell your version of the first time we said, "I love you" to each other.
- Retell your version of the proposal.
- Retell your version of our wedding day.

Place one slip of paper under your cups, plates, and napkins. As each slip of paper is discovered, enjoy retelling these chapters in your relationship story.

Our Memory Game Prior to the date, make your own memory game by selecting 20–25 of your favorite pictures of events in your relationship. Print two copies of each picture (40–50 pictures total). To play, take turns flipping over two pictures, searching for a match. When you get a match, share a memory associated with that picture.

A Walk Down Our Memory Lane Anniversary Date (continued)

A Blast from Our Past Repeat an activity that you did on your first date, or one from one of your early dates (this may take some creativity to come up with an at-home modification).

Treats For dessert, eat a treat that you had together early in your dating.

Start the Conversation
When did you first know that you loved me?
What is your favorite memory of us?
How do you envision us 50 years from now?

Card Bowling & Dessert

(A fun variation of a traditional date! Works great as a group date!)

Card Bowling Bring a deck of cards with you to a bowling alley. Before you begin bowling, assign a specific form of bowling to each suit. For example:

    Spade = Bowl right-handed
    Diamond = Bowl left-handed
    Club = Bowl professional style
    Heart = Bowl with your eyes closed

Prior to each roll, draw a card from the deck. Bowl in the way assigned to the suit. (Based on our experience with this, you might want to put the bumpers up ☺.)

Card Dessert For dessert, go to a grocery store or fast food restaurant and select four dessert options that appeal to you. Assign each to a suit. For example:

    Spade: Ice cream carton
    Diamond: Ice cream bars
    Club: Ice cream sandwiches
    Heart: Root beer floats

Whoever won the game of bowling draws a card to determine what the dessert will be. Bring the dessert home (or enjoy it at the restaurant) and play a card game.

Start the Conversation
What would people be surprised to learn about you?

Dinner Drawn Out of a Hat

(Adding an element of chance in determining your three-course meal adds a new layer of fun to going out to eat!)

Name Your Places Write the names of several restaurants or food establishments (at least three total) in your area on individual pieces of paper. For convenience, consider selecting places that are geographically close to each other and that won't require a tip, such as fast casual restaurants or fast food restaurants. Go for variety!

Dinner Drawn Out of a Hat Put all of the slips of paper in a hat. Draw a paper from the hat to determine where you will go to get an appetizer. Enjoy conversing as you drive to that place and eat your appetizer. Then draw a paper from the hat to determine the location for the main course. Go and enjoy. Repeat this a third time for your dessert to cap off the date.

Start the Conversation
If you could obtain information about one thing in your future, what would you want to know?

If tomorrow morning you could wake up possessing a new ability or attribute, what would you want it to be?

Your World of Books Date

(How much fun can you have in a bookstore? You may be surprised! If you don't have access to a bookstore with enough genres of books to do these activities, adapt this for a library.)

Childhood Each of you find one of your favorite books from when you were a young child. Share with each other why you enjoyed the books you selected and memories associated with them.

Take Me Back to School Each of you find a book that you had to read in junior high or high school. Share what you remember about reading the book and discussing it in class.

Heroes Each of you find a biography or autobiography about an individual from history or an individual who is living that you admire. Find a paragraph or page with interesting information to share. Discuss what you admire about that person.

World Records Find books containing world records. Try to impress each other with the randomness or impressiveness of the world records that you find.

Vacation Destinations Each of you find a book that references a destination you want to travel to together. Share what you find and discuss why you selected this destination.

A Personal Interest Each of you find a book on a topic that you're interested in reading or learning about. Share what you find and discuss why you have interest in that topic.

Your World of Books Date (continued)

A Little Humor Look through joke books and find some stellar (or cheesy) jokes. Share them together and have a good laugh!

Treats Some bookstores contain small bakeries, so consider purchasing something there. Or, get sundaes after you leave the bookstore.

Start the Conversation
What were your reading habits as a child?
What was the worst book you had to read for school?
What was the best book?
What are your top 5 books?
What book has had the biggest influence on your life? In what ways?